INSTAGRAM BUSINESS:

How to Know the secrets to create a real business with instagram. How to use social network and exploit all its power.

Table of Contents

Introduction

Instagram is a social networking service for sharing photos and videos that were originally created for smartphones. Since its founding in 2010, the platform has become hugely popular, especially among millennials.

Leveraging Instagram for Business Marketing

Leveraging Instagram content for your business is actually not much different than using any typical channels that you would otherwise utilize. The same principles apply. You must be sure to know your audience and know what they are going to be attracted to. When you have done this, what will happen is your audience will naturally come your way and that will help your business grow. There are some things you can to do make it happen though, and when you effectively leverage Instagram for your business, this can lead to some incredible profitability. Here are some tips to make Instagram work effectively for you.

Consistency is a Critical Key to Success

The thing about Instagram like all social media is that consistency is vitally important. Make sure that you create a theme and that you stick with the theme. You should only post on Instagram once per day, and while business owners that do not have social media managers may find this cumbersome, if you developed the content calendar, you will have Instagram stuff locked and ready to go for the day.

Next, understand that there are two types of content – there is your personal content and your business content. If you go on a vacation and you see something on vacation that is connected to your business but would be on brand for you, post it. Of course, make sure that your followers expect it. For example, you should always post at the same time of day. So, if you like the idea of posting at noon, have things ready to go by then. Be mindful that your visuals are your brand. So, back to the vacation idea, you should not be posting photos of you in a swimsuit on the beach if your business is something that is completely unrelated – this would give your customers the impression that you are not professional.

Use Call to Action Content Every Time

Calls to action are vitally important for making sales, this means that if you are posting something and there is nothing for the person to do, then your post is not successful. For example, if you have an e-commerce store for jewelry and you are posting about your wares, the best thing to do is have a link in your bio and a call to action telling customers that they should click on your bio link above to see the piece of jewelry along with others on your e-commerce site. This is a call to action that can be put on the Instagram image or it can be embedded in the caption. Either way, a call to action is essential for any sales copy, and Instagram, although it is images, traffics in sales copy.

Have Contests on Your Instagram Feed

A great way to get people to give you their e-mail addresses and or other contact information is through a contest. Here's the thing – you may need to give away something in order to get more back in return. Let's go back to the jewelry store that was referenced above. Maybe you do a giveaway for a nice bracelet but what people need to do to get in the drawing is click on the link taking them to a landing page for them to submit their e-mail address. This is a really easy way to capture leads. The best part is people could end up browsing on the site and purchase items, or you could use that e-mail list for promotions and in turn that could result in someone coming back to your site and making a purchase. Ultimately, these contests end up paying for themselves in terms of profit margin and the little bit you needed to do in order to get the lead.

Use Instagram Stories to Breathe Life into Your Product

When people tag you with their use of your products then what you can do is repost and give them their time in the sun because they are promoting you. This will gain you lots of credibility because there is nothing more that followers enjoy like being a featured person or account of someone they are into. That being said, the Story is a great way to make this really work and then some. Encourage your followers to post Instagram stories of them with your product or talking about your service and how it has changed their lives. This is a really simple way for your followers to show how much they love what you do and a great way to connect with new customers. You can also use stories to showcase things that you are doing for customers as well. So, if you are developing a new product or service, the story is a great way to peel back the curtain and build excitement as people are gearing up for a launch day. When these stories are well done, there is a better than good chance that they will end up going viral – and that is something your business will always love.

Use the Influence of Influencers

There are many people who wish they could be Instagram influencers and then there are actual influencers. This is a network that you really want to tap into, but don't just try and get a big time celebrity or Instagram influencer to tout what you do – seek out someone who has real credibility with the audience that you are seeking or someone within your industry. This is the type of targeted influence that can help you get to the next level with your products and services. In fact, as you start working with influencers you will notice an uptick on the activity on your Instagram account. This is a simple way to appreciate everything that influencers can do for you and your business. Having influencers steer their followers towards you is a great investment as well. The best influencers know that you are willing to pay a premium, so while it is smart to develop a good relationship with them, understand they are not going to post your content for free unless it is something that can add value for them. Any time you can provide value for these influencers, it is definitely something that you want to do. At the end of the day, Instagram influencers that do the job right are great allies to have on your behalf as you are growing your business – especially if you are a start up company.

Chapter 1. Benefits of using Instagram for marketing

There are many advantages of using Instagram for your marketing purposes. It provides chances for your business and avenues that you might not have gotten with any other strategies. Let's look at some of those benefits.

Visual appeal

The very essence of Instagram is the visual appeal. The network is all about images and videos that appeal to its audience. You can communicate with your audience through images, which are better in the long run than written content.

Photos tend to encourage more engagement than written content. It is easier for the audience to see and understand and takes much less of their time.

Instagram also lets you test out different forms of images and find out which one's appeal most to the audience. You can then use these on other channels such as your website or blog and email newsletters.

The photo sharing ability for Instagram enables you to showcase your product in a creative manner.

If you can come up with great content for your Instagram feed, it could change your whole business and increase sales for you in the long run.

Large Audience

Instagram provides you with an extremely large audience who are also potential clients. With over 150 million active users, it gives a rather impressive possibility for your business. Imagine that, being able to market your business to millions of people all at once.

It is easier than traditional marketing where the audience can see your photos at once. Compare it to a billboard you put up where only people who drive by the area can see it, and only those not distracted by one thing or the other.

Instagram on the other hand allows your audience to view the image and they can hardly miss it on their feed. They are also not limited by geographic location or time.

The app is also great for when you are expanding to branches across the world, as it has users all over the world. This allows you to market internationally, with just one marketing campaign. You can do it all from a central location without ever having stepped in some of the areas your audience is from.

The use of hash tags allows you to increase your audience, as more people can access your content through the hash tag.

More Engagement

Instagram has quite a high engagement rate. When running a marketing campaign, you want your audience to be as engaging as possible, at that moment and in future too.

To generate engagement on Instagram is quite easy as all you would need is to follow those people who talk about your brand, comment on and like another users' content. Using hash tags also allows you to facilitate conversation. You can have the users contribute to a topic by asking a question.

The community you build on Instagram is likely to engage more often because they will see your content regularly. Unlike a post on a blog where they must go to your blog to see additional content,

Instagram lets your followers see content by you on their feed if they are already on the app.

Such constant engagement ensures that your customers will come back for repeat purchases. That when one buys from your brand, and they see it again several times, the next time they need something that you offer, they will most likely buy from your brand again.

Increased engagement also makes it easier to introduce new products to your audience.

Storytelling Ability

Creating your brand on Instagram can take up different forms. The app allows you to create a story behind your products. Through posts on the stories feature, you can show your audience some behind-the –scenes images and videos. Have them relate to your brand by introducing your staff and maybe even yourself to them.

You can also have images that show your clients the products in real life situations, create a lifestyle with your brand. Tell the audience a story through the different Instagram features.

Keep Tabs on Competition

Instagram gives you the ability to see what other businesses in your industry are doing. By following the hash tags that are like your own will show you how the others in the industry are promoting their brands.

Get ideas from them on how better to market your products and stay ahead.

Free Marketing from users

This is the ideal kind of marketing that any business would love to have. It is made possible by Instagram through User Generated Content. Remember that your audience is also creating and sharing content of their own.

If you post user generated content, you may be able to tap into a different audience other than those who follow you. It is also a great way to connect with your audience and interact even more.

By having the users add a hash tag generated by you to their posts, they market your business and in return, you can pick one of their posts to add to your feed and give them a shout out.

There are many more benefits to using Instagram for marketing, all of which you will gain once you start using the medium.

Chapter 2. Choosing a Niche and Setting Up

Before you can start to make a massive splash on Instagram Stories though, you first need to get started with regular old Instagram.

And now it's time to reveal the power of Instagram and how you can tap into it. It's time to learn what it is about Instagram that makes massive stars and just why brands are willing to invest so much of their money into it...

Selling the Dream

Selling the Dream

In business, there is a very useful term that it pays to understand. That term is 'Value Proposition'.

The value proposition is the way in which you are claiming to offer value to your users. This means that you're asking what it is about your products, your services or your content that makes people interested. How do their lives stand to improve through their interaction with you?

This is all about understanding that the total should always be more than the sum of its parts. In other words, you are not selling the brick and mortar – the physical materials that go into the creation of your product.

If you are selling a book on getting fit, then you are not really selling a book on fitness. Rather, you are selling fitness itself. You are selling the feeling of having amazing abs. Of knowing that you look great when you take your top off. Of knowing that you are desirable. You are selling the feeling of waking up first thing in the morning full of energy and ready to go. You are selling the feeling of looking *great* in your clothes. Of taking up physical space thanks to your muscle. Of walking into a room and making an impression and turning heads. Those are all amazing things to be able to sell someone and your audience will be willing to pay a *big* price for that.

The same goes for business consultancy. You aren't just selling information: you're selling the dream of

running a highly successful business: of wearing slick suits, of having employees and of knowing that what you're doing is important.
 Your value proposition is your 'dream'. It's the dream that people are willing to pay money for and it's the dream that will set your business apart from the competition. The dream is what will turn followers into true fans and what will get you likes and shares and follows.

And Instagram is *all about* selling dreams.
 Remember what we said earlier: Instagram is about finding art in everyday activities. It's about taking something that is relatively dull and making it seem incredibly exciting.
 People will often follow others on Instagram because they want to live vicariously and to be inspired.

Examples of Highly Effective Instagram Accounts

Examples of Highly Effective Instagram Accounts

Take a look at some of the most popular fitness brands and how they operate. These channels work by posting images of a perfect fitness lifestyle. You'll see silhouettes of people running against a sunset along a beach. You'll see pictures of incredibly ripped guys standing over weights with chalk in their hands.

You'll see pictures of incredibly fit women with perfectly formed rears in the squatting rack.

All of these things paint a picture that is highly desirable for anyone who wishes they were a bit fitter. They love looking at these images – especially if they aren't that happy with their own fitness – because they find them inspiring and because they like to imagine that one day their lives will be like that.

That's also why fashion is so popular on Instagram. There are countless female Instagram stars who post pictures of themselves in highly form-fitting outfits, looking absolutely stunning and thereby making other women highly jealous (of course they also tend to have a few male followers as well!).

And can you imagine what kind of position that puts these women in when it comes to promoting products? With all those followers who wish their lives were just like those women's, their ability to promote a product is of course almost unparalleled!

Another very popular type of account is the 'Battlestation' channel. Battlestations are essentially setups for gaming PCs or productivity stations. These are super powerful desktop PCs with advanced lighting set-ups, multi-monitor arrays, keyboards with insane lighting and awesome pop-culture décor. Again, people like to follow these channels as fans of tech because they can use them for ideas, inspiration and a little bit of lust.

What about food porn? These accounts literally just take photos of beautiful looking meals and combine this with recipe advice, or reviews of places to eat. Again though, this appeals to the kind of person who loves cooking and loves eating and who gets a real kick out of making something delicious or finding those hidden indie places to eat.

Travel is another area that lends itself very naturally to these kinds of channels and it's not uncommon to see people posting pictures of themselves in front of lots of exotic locations. While they come in many different forms, the best Instagram accounts are all about promoting a way of life, a movement or a dream – and that is where the incredible engagement comes from.

If you want an example of how Instagram can work in the extreme, then consider 'stunting'. Stunting is the somewhat strange practice of essentially pretending that you have more money than you do, or that you live an incredibly rich lifestyle.

A typical example might be to take a photo of your own hand on a car steering wheel. That car is of course a Lamborghini and just to complete the image, you are also wearing a Rolex. Other people will withdraw lots of their own cash, so they can lie in bed along with lots of piles of it, or they will take photos of themselves on first class flights (when actually they were just passing through to go to the toilet).

People who wish they were better off and who dream of this kind of lifestyle will then often follow those accounts, just so that they can live vicariously and imagine that it is them with all that money.

Sometimes, they will even *know* that the 'stunter' is faking it and won't even care because they are just happy to see those images and to pretend along with the creator.

It's a strange practice but it just shows the magic of Instagram and what a powerful impact that can have...

Choosing Your Niche

To get started then and to start doing the same, you're going to first have to choose the niche you want to focus on. A niche of course is a subject matter and it can also mean your industry. A niche means more than that though because it also defines who your audience is, what the value proposition is and more. As you can imagine, certain niches will lend themselves a little better to Instagram than others. We've seen just how effective fitness can be as a niche and how other things like fashion, food and more all work well too.

Of course though, it can pay to try and avoid competing directly within a massive niche. While it is still outlandishly high, engagement has been going *down* somewhat on Instagram as numbers have risen and the obvious reason for that, is that the more people are on the platform, the harder it is to stand out and make a splash.

If you want to sidestep direct competition, then try choosing a smaller niche within the broader category. So for instance, if you are going to tackle fitness, then you can always try going with something slightly different or more specific – like fitness for the elderly, outdoor fitness, weight lifting, calisthenics etc.

Likewise, if you are going to choose 'fashion', then maybe you could focus more on plus side fashion, on retro fashion, on 'fashion on a budget' etc. By giving your brand something more distinct to help it stand out, you will find that more people want to follow you and that you make a bigger impact as a result.

For Existing Brands

Of course, there's a good chance that you already *have* your brand and that you're just looking for a way to promote that brand *through* Instagram. In this case, you want to consider how you can take whatever your industry or niche is and then make it into something a little more visual and inspiring.

For example, if you happen to be in Life Insurance, then you might be wondering just how you can make that as inspiring and visual as something like fitness. The good news is that there *is* a way – you just need to choose a theme that is highly related, that will appeal to the precise same audience, but that isn't necessarily directly the same as your product.

 Ask yourself: what is the value proposition of your business and how can you portray that in a visual way?
 There are essentially two value propositions when it comes to life insurance. Those are:
 ☐ Looking after your family
 ☐ Improving your finances

You can focus on either of these for your Instagram account. Either you could post lots of pictures of happy families in nice houses doing things together, or you could post lots of pictures related to money saving and living a cost-effective lifestyle.

 Either of these accounts would give people a good reason to follow and would potentially be inspiring but neither is *directly* on the nose.

Another option is to choose a 'personal brand'. A personal brand is essentially where you take your own persona and make that into an indistinguishable part of your company. You become the public face and you bond with your audience by allowing them to feel as though they are getting to know you.

In many ways, Richard Branson is a personal brand. Likewise, you can also think of a lot of top bloggers and vloggers (think PewDiePie or Tim Ferriss) as being personal brands.

The great thing about a personal brand is that people become fans of *you* and not just the product or service that you're promoting. From there, it is then your job to demonstrate that you 'live what you preach'. Your personal brand and your lifestyle match what your product is about.

So if you have a blog about fitness and you have a personal brand, then your posts can be of you working out, of you eating healthy meals, of you going on healthy walks... etc.

But the difference here is that you're also going to occasionally include photos that are more related to your personal life: maybe photos of you out and about with your friends, or photos of your other hobbies or your dog. If you get this right and if you've built enough of a relationship with your followers, then they will like getting these insights into your life and they will all become part of your image.

Note that a personal brand works very well for Instagram Stories which have that very personal and intimate feel. If you don't currently have a personal brand, then you might want to consider exposing yourself a little more to your audience for the purposes of this new tool.

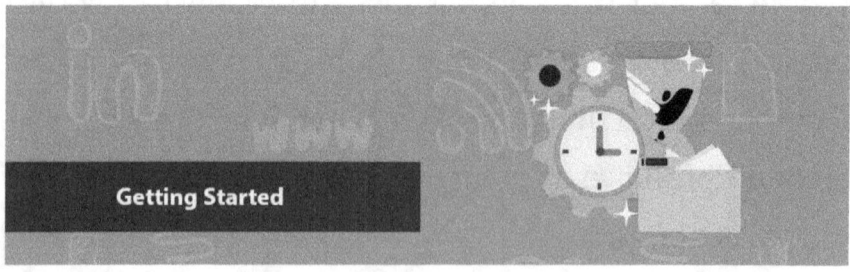

Getting Started

Getting Started

Once you've chosen how you're going to approach Instagram, all that is left to do is to get started with an account.

For all of the recent additions and innovations to Instagram, one thing is missing: and that is the inclusion of any kind of website. While there is a website to be found (www.instagram.com), it is very limited in scope. You can scroll through your homefeed on here and you can like photos and videos. What you can't do though, is to upload photos.

For that, you're going to need the phone app for iOS, Android or Windows Phone. Using this, you'll be able to sign up and create an account (or use your existing Facebook account) and from there, posting photos is a simple matter of hitting the 'Plus' icon in the middle down the bottom and then choosing a photo from your gallery or taking a new one with the camera. There's also the option to record a new video here.

Once the photo is taken or uploaded, you can then add filters, edit the photo and write comments underneath. It's all very self-explanatory, so we won't go into it in a lot of detail here. Congratulations, you're now on

Instagram and you're now ready to start building a massive following and creating some real trust and influence!

Chapter 3. How to Develop a Content Strategy

This chapter will cover the broad aspects of your content strategy on Instagram: what you should be doing with your feed, what you definitely should not be doing, and what types of content have been successful on Instagram in the past.

What You Should Be Doing

The key to doing this is to remain active. Set up a schedule for your content and stick with it.

The top brands on Instagram post around 6 times per week. That adds up to more than 300 posts per year, which sounds very exhausting. However, frequent and high-quality posts are essential to maintaining visibility and engagement.

For people to discover your feed, it needs to have visibility. This means, if you do not have an active following yet, you need to be posting new and interesting content with regularity. Your older posts will not stay relevant in your follower's feeds, and will certainly not show up in the hashtag feeds that you need to be in if you want to grow your following.

Furthermore, posting content regularly is essential if you want to maintain your existing following. It's definitely true that most users don't clean out their subscriptions that often, but when they do, you surely want to be remembered as an important part of your follower's daily feed. Maintaining a regular schedule of content keeps your followers engaged, and therefore, they're more likely to remain your followers in the future.

Aside from this, make sure you keep all of your information in your bio and links up to date. Don't forget to update your information if you change your website, corporate identity, or location. Putting out inaccurate information is a surefire way to lose current and potential followers.

Things You Should Not Be Doing

While it is important to remain active with your account, it is equally important not to be too active. People on Instagram are looking for genuine, authentic content that they will not find on other social media platforms like Facebook. Do not treat Instagram like just another marketing platform. If you are only posting pictures of your product, people will be turned off and will not become followers.

Instead, you should be posting honest, interesting things that attract attention without being obvious advertisements. If you want to post pictures of a new product, tease it, don't show the whole thing. Give tidbits using interesting framing to build curiosity and engagement. The Instagram audience primarily consists of a young lot that wants quirky, interesting content that they can engage with.

Posting too frequently can also spam your follower's feed with content. And when you forcibly occupy too much of your follower's feeds with low quality, obvious marketing content, there is a high risk of being unfollowed.

You should also focus on not getting discouraged. Do not expect to get a million followers overnight. Building a network takes time and luck. If you stick to your account and develop high-quality posts, eventually you will have a breakthrough. Furthermore, do not allow negative feedback to discourage you. While Instagram does have auto-moderation features, they will not catch every inappropriate or unfortunate comment on your posts. Take criticism constructively, do not allow it to tear down your work. Instead, use it to improve your future posts. At the same time, recognize that not all forms of criticism are valid.

Developing Content Pillars

In making your long-term plan for Instagram success, you should decide on a number of 'content pillars' that will make up a majority of your posts on the platform. To start with, you should probably decide on three or four pillars to start building your brand. Pillars are the foundation of your brand on Instagram, the things people expect to see from you in their feed.

Your goal should be to develop a consistent identity for your profile on Instagram. Focus on what you want people to think about when they hear your brand name, and how you can build that image in their minds. When planning content pillars, you should focus on a consistent brand image while maintaining sufficient variety to maintain interest without diluting that brand identity.

Go through that section to identify relevant posts that are suited to your marketing goals and use that as a foundation for your initial content pillars.

Of course, even though this is how you are starting out, you do not need to restrict yourself. As you build your following, you'll be able to identify what works for your audience and what does not. Plus, your marketing goals may change over time which means you might have to adopt a new strategy. So, don't be afraid to change your strategy in the long run.

Scheduling Content

Part of maintaining a regular content schedule is to maintain a content calendar. Make a regular schedule for what type of posts your audience would like. Throw in some variety and don't repeat the same kind of posts every week. If you have a regular feature that routinely generates high engagement, schedule it more often and set a particular day or time for it so that your followers know more about your routine.

Having a schedule ahead of time can also reduce the burden of keeping up with your feed. You can 'pre-bake' a number of posts ahead of time. That is, set up a number of potential posts in a single session, then release them according to your schedule. If you have a reserve of pre-baked content, this can allow you to keep up with your scheduled content even if unexpected events prevent you from creating new content on the fly.

When it comes to scheduling content, you should be aware of optimal posting timings. Statistics have shown in the past that the highest engagement on Instagram posts are on Monday and Thursday between 8 AM and 9 AM Eastern Standard Time. In general, Monday and Thursday are high engagement times of the week outside of the 3 PM to 4 PM window, though any work-day outside of normal office hours tends to result in higher post engagement than during work hours or weekends.

You should keep these timings in mind when planning your content schedule, along with the time zone you are targeting. If you are planning for a nationwide American reach, Eastern Standard is ideal, while if your scope is more local, you should target the same time window within your local time zone.

A Few Examples of Successful Post Types

Now, we are about to cover a number of successful content examples that can be used as the foundation for your content pillars. This list is not intended to be exhaustive and we acknowledge that you might have a super great idea that no one may have executed before. However, if you're taking baby steps in the world of Instagram marketing, some of these options are a good way to start.

Behind the Scenes

One great way to use the distinctive aspects of Instagram is to post great 'behind the scenes' images, videos, and stories. The goal of this type of content is to give your followers a more intimate look into how your business operates and what it represents when compared with more sterile, traditional marketing materials.

Highlight the way your team goes about its daily routine, the process of putting your product or service together, the fun moments that emerge in breaks. Consider creating a 'day-in-the-life' through the 'stories' function. Showing your followers how the sausage is made, so to speak, will make them feel like you are giving them inside information that is otherwise inaccessible. This feeling of exclusivity can generate further interest and boost engagement.

Employee Reposts

Keep track of whether your team members have Instagram accounts, and engage with them directly if they do. Follow your team members on the platform and encourage them to follow you. Keep an eye out for high quality or potentially high engagement content posted by your employees.

Adding content to your feed this way has several benefits. First, if you have creative and energetic employees who naturally create high-quality social media posts on their own, reposting and commenting on their content is a much hassle-free way to add more content to your own feed. This content will feel 'authentic' as it was not created as a part of an active marketing campaign.

Second, engaging with your employees directly can build engagement and community within your organization, with potential ancillary benefits for morale. Finally, involving your team members in your social media outreach can convert them into ambassadors for your brand, even if marketing isn't part of their day-to-day responsibilities.

Follower Reposts

Building engagement with your followers is not a one-way street. If you want people to engage with you, you need to engage with them. Keep track of your mentions and the use of hashtags through your notifications and Instagram analytics.

Reply to their comments, like positive comments, comment or like on reposts, etcetera. If your followers know that you are watching, they are more likely to engage with you in the future.

Educational Posts

Many successful Instagram brands use educational materials as a major content pillar. Your followers are more likely to engage with content that will benefit them.

'Educational' content can take a lot of different forms. If your business is food related, it could be a recipe, tips on how to get that same great taste, or how to use your product in a familiar or creative dish. If your product is more technical, you could post detailed 'how to use it' posts and provide a breakdown of useful features. However, educational posts do not need to be directly related to your specific goods or services. You can post informative content about the marketplace or news that influence your field of business-like statistics, poll results, profit figures, and so forth.

Educational content can generate high engagement because it includes a 'call to action.' If you have posted a recipe or a how-to guide, it gives your followers clear instructions on how to use your products. This produces high engagement because it encourages your followers to make you a part of their lives outside of just watching your feed.

Educational content can also be an avenue for people to discover your feed, especially if you are posting facts and statistics about your field of business. While Instagram is certainly not a primary source for people doing research online, people may still search for facts and figures about things related to your business or see the facts and figures you've posted in a hashtag feed and want to learn more.

'Piggybacking' on Influencers

Follow influencers on Instagram who interact with your business space. If you own a restaurant, follow famous chefs and their businesses. If you sell sporting goods, follow athletes. If you are a photographer, follow famous photographers and outlets that highlight high-quality photography like *National Geographic.* If your account is all about fashion, follow prominent labels and high influence fashion profiles.

Keep an eye on what high influence accounts are posting. Interacting with a high influence account is one of the easiest ways to expose your handle to people who aren't following you yet. Repost content from high influence feeds that you follow. Comment on their high-quality posts. Highlight any example of an influencer mentioning or using your product or service. Even if they neglect to mention it themselves.

By inserting yourself into the feeds of high exposure accounts that are related to what you do, you increase the chances of your handle being noticed by potential followers who are already interested in things related to your business line.

'Piggybacking' on News, Trends, or Events

Keep an eye on the calendar for current events. Watch the 'top posts' feed through Instagram's discover function to identify high engagement and trending hashtags. You should keep an eye out for hot trends, news events, or holiday that relates to your business line.

There is a holiday for just about everything these days. Make a list of holidays that are relevant to your business and make sure you post about them. If a trend or news event is closely related to what you do, do not miss an opportunity to point it out. Trends can tell you what people are thinking about. If you can jump on a trend, it will increase chances of visibility, boost engagement with potential followers, allowing you to earn a couple of new followers.

Fun Stuff

Posting fun content, like 'boomerang' animations, memes, and funny behind-the-scenes moments is a great way to make your posts stand out.

Business Culture Posts

One reason you may be on Instagram is to highlight your business culture. If you have a slogan or a distinctive business philosophy, you should highlight it. The standard format for something like this would be a solid color or otherwise simple background with high contrast block text over the top, similar to the formatting for 'meme' posts.

'Take-overs'

One common strategy for high-engagement stories content is a 'take-over.' In general, this means handing over control of your Instagram account to somebody other than your dedicated social media specialist for a set period of time. Typically, you would want this person to create a series of posts through the temporary 'stories' feature.

You could do an employee take-over as a more extensive form of behind-the-scenes content. In other words, 'see what Martha from sales does in a day of work.' You could do a follower take-over, in which one of your followers showcases how they use your product throughout a typical day. Like reposting content from employees or followers, this is a low-effort way of creating highly authentic, engaging content.

Obviously, you want to be careful with this type of post, and you should only give temporary control of a social media account to a trusted employee or follower who you are confident will represent the brand well.

Chapter 4. Why Instagram Is Important for Employers

You may have some questions at this point. Why go through all this effort to post a few times on social media? Is it actually going to help my business, or am I just wasting my time? You have to keep in mind that, while social media has a lot of people floating around and a lot of big-time users, it takes time to build a following. Gaining followers isn't an overnight process, but if you continue to promote your profile, it will make your business more profitable.

The more comfortable your business becomes with using Instagram and other social media platforms, the more productive you will become. Online businesses are becoming more popular every day. The fact of the matter is, the less that people have to shop around, the better it is for them. Being able to give your customers what they are looking for up front and supplying them with the option to avoid looking into other businesses is a way to create an immediate conversion. You want your followers to promote your company name and buy products from your business alone. Search engines have allowed people to find a huge variety of companies by what they are searching for. Now, social media has developed the same capabilities. It's the perfect place to build your company's reputation and promote sales from your page.

The Future in Internet Marketing

If you're still not convinced that internet marketing and social media platforms are the way to go, then you need to think about the future. Online marketing has already become very dominant on the scene, but by the time the year 2020 comes around, more and more people will be using their mobile phones and handheld tablets to do the majority of their shopping. When physical printing becomes obsolete, the online market will be the only thing left.

Now is the time to be perfecting your skills in internet marketing, especially in the realm of social media. Over the next few years, Generation Z will be growing up, and they will become the major consumers of the era. Since this generation grew up surrounded by technology, they were raised with YouTube videos and smartphones instead of TV advertisements and magazines. They have entirely different priorities than the generations before them, but they also have a different way of looking at life. Due to the fact that they are raised with technology, they never have to wait for much and have instant access to whatever they need, including buying things online. Generation Z is referred to as having an 8-second filter, which they use to find content that they care about and actually want to look at. They don't have to waste any time scrolling through loads of information when they can just bypass it by finding exactly what they want.

Companies are now having to figure out how to capture the attention of this generation and keep them focused on the product being sold within an 8 second time frame before they move on. If they can't capture their attention and hold it, the sale will be bypassed and they will move on to the next segment of their news feeds. However, it isn't just this generation that is turning to technology for shopping. More and more businesses are closing their physical doors due to online shoppers. Warehouses are limitless in terms of the internet, and people don't have to wait in line to get what they want. Shopping online has become as easy as clicking three buttons and tapping the screen to pay for something online. With the age of online shopping on the rise, marketers need to be prepared to keep up.

In order for companies to stay profitable in a constantly changing technological world, they need to be able to focus on the trending topics and platforms of that moment. Advertising on Facebook used to make major waves because that was the platform where most people were looking and making friends. You could follow company pages and that would be enough. However, now Instagram has become the most popular social media platform for people; it offers a wide variety of photo and filter options, story abilities, and other features that the other social media platforms don't have. By advertising and building marketing strategies for Instagram, there is the option to create a quick and easy link directly to the company website that's posting the ad. The posts also don't stand out as ads right away, but look similar to any other Instagram post until you notice the "swipe up" banner at the bottom that will take you to the shopping site.

The Internet is the future of all resources. Marketing is becoming entirely digital and is moving away from physical print due to the fact that fewer people are buying anything physically printed. With practically everyone online in the social media world, selling a product has never been easier. Instagram users are not only more engaged, but they are also usually online shoppers. A study recently showed that 72% of Instagram users made a purchase decision after seeing something advertised on Instagram. The most common categories that saw sales were clothing, makeup, shoes, and jewelry. Instagram shoppers are easy to convert when it comes to sales because they know what they are looking for in products. They are following the brands they like, and as they discover new trends in their newsfeed, they continue to buy new products that suit them. That's why Instagram is so high on the charts for influencer marketing. People are following beauty bloggers and trend setters that have unique styles because they want to be on the same path as they follow their brand ambassadors' advice on what to buy and what to wear.

Internet marketing has become more prominent in recent years due to the fact that people are buying more products online than they are from physical stores. Through social media, and Instagram in particular, it's becoming easier to go from advertisement to webpage with the swipe of a finger.

There are different banners that can be displayed on advertisements, including ones that say "Learn More" or "Shop Now" at the bottom of the picture. These allow you to simply swipe the line upward, and it will automatically load the business website for you from the advertisement you were looking at.

Chapter 5. How to Build Your Brand on Instagram

You need to see your business, initiative or project as a brand.

You need to see it as something that is marketable and something the world needs to see and invest in. You need to take your venturing into Instagram as seriously as possible. When you take something seriously, you will be compelled to put all of your effort into it. That's how you should see your blog because that is what it is. You have a brand, and in order for it to be successful, it needs to have a noticeable impact on the Instagram community. In order for this to happen, you need to build on your brand. What does that mean? It means that you will take to developing your business from a personal and business point of view. By constantly raising awareness of your brand and what you have to offer, you are building your brand. You can make use of campaign tactics and strategies to increase awareness of your brand.

This chapter has provided profiles on a couple of the most successful brands on Instagram. In these profiles, you will find information on what these brands do, the reasons behind their success and what you can learn from them so your brand can be successful on Instagram, too.

One thing you will notice about these brands is that their respective niches are either highly competitive or challenging when it comes to finding a target audience. But they've taken such curveballs, and they have made them work in their favor. None of these brands are the first to do what they do, but they've managed to carve their own path in their respective niches. This is no easy feat. You will find that ,as you go through their profiles, you will be inspired or moved to do more for your brand. You will get a better understanding about building your brand on Instagram and seeing your blog as a business–regardless of what the blog may be about.

If your blog belongs to a niche that is highly saturated, or a niche that has a target audience that may not be easy to tap into, you will find ways to navigate through these changes, and who knows, maybe someone will use your brand as an example for successful brands on Instagram.

Examples of Real Cases

Califia Farms (@califiafarms)

Who Are They?

Califia Farms is a brand known for producing and selling beverages that are made from natural ingredients. Their beverage products range from coffees to milk and juices. The beverages are bottled in uniquely-shaped, and creatively designed, packaging. Califia Farms received top honors in the global packaging design category from the *Beverage World Magazine* awards. This brand was also recognized as one of the most successful brands on Instagram by top Internet Marketing Company HubSpot.

Califia Farms uses Instagram to showcase their innovatively-designed and eye-catching packaging. The brand has amassed just under 70,000 followers on Instagram, with a significant amount of them engaging with the blog on a regular basis.

Why Are They Successful?

You can tell that Califia Farms' success is not accidental. There are tactics and strategies that they applied in order to harness their audience and gain the success they have achieved. Their strategies required a great amount of thinking and planning. These are the major aspects they focused and worked on in order to appeal to their target audience and build their brand:

Their content is aesthetically pleasing. It appeals to the viewers' senses. Califia Farms' Instagram blog is known for having beautiful, high quality images. Every image is strategically curated and captured. Whether the bottle is the focal point of the image or if it serves as an accessory in the image, the beverage product is depicted in a context that is appealing to the brand's target audience: physically active users who are seeking to maintain a healthy lifestyle. Califia Farms has managed to strike a balance between posting relatable content and promoting their product at the same time. Viewers don't feel like they are being overwhelmed with spam-like content.

Every Califia Farms product is captured against a simple backdrop–be it indoors or outdoors. Typical backgrounds you'll find in their images are countertop surfaces, aisles in stores, or natural, green backgrounds. Their posts are visually consistent–they unify one another.

One takes pleasure in perusing the Califia Farms blog on Instagram because they know that their eyes are in for a treat. The brand also makes use of innovative creative concepts in their photos; every post contains a different concept or idea. Every post gives one a sense of enjoyment and activity–they make the viewer want to be active and indulge in the beverages.

When someone looks at a post uploaded by Califia Farms, they aren't just satisfied visually. The posts have a way of appealing to your sense of taste and sense of smell. You will feel like eating or drinking what is displayed in the content. You will feel as if you can smell the flavors of the beverage in the image.

When you look at every post, you can tell that time and care were taken to create the images. The product wasn't just carelessly placed against a backdrop. They make use of design concepts such as lighting, symmetry and value to ensure that their content is a design dream. The Califia Farms Instagram blog exudes originality because that is exactly what their content is–original. You can tell that their ideas are their own.

Their content is lively. The brand isn't just known for uploading images that are attractive or appealing. Videos and GIFs can be found on the blog as well. These are part of the brand's trademark and their overall message which is about being healthy and being active. They depict this through videos and GIFs that are lively and playful in nature. The brand often uses videos as a means to teach their followers how to make certain products–like steaming non-dairy milk, for example. Instead of loading the videos with information that could come across as boring, Califia Farms makes their videos fun and interactive–which results in engagement with followers. The videos are also curated carefully in order to pass the main message whilst appealing to the followers' visual senses. You can tell that they took time to plan the videos in order to execute them perfectly.

The use of videos and GIFs gives the blog an active vibe. It is also a nifty way of diversifying the kind of content they give their followers. Instead of continuously uploading static images, they went the extra mile to ensure that their content expresses the fun and active agenda they are trying to pass.

Sometimes they upload videos for the sole purpose of entertaining their followers. The videos won't contain any tangible information the followers need to capture, but the videos sure are fun to watch.

Keeping content diverse keeps followers entertained and eagerly anticipating what's going to come next. When you ask a follower about the brand, they will be able to give you a clear description of what the brand is about. This is because of the brand's consistency and creativity when it comes to the content they upload.

They make good use of their captions. Califia Farms' creativity overflows into the captions they add to the images, videos and GIFs they upload. Captions are an important part of an Instagram blog, and this brand definitely did not neglect that. They've used their captions to their advantage as well. Every caption is specific to the post it accompanies.

Since they know that the majority of their followers are under the age of 30, the colloquialisms used in the captions and the style in which the captions are written give the captions a youthful vibe. They address the audience in their captions as if they are talking to their friends–which allows the audience to connect with the brand on a personal level.

The captions are also specific to the post they accompany. Every caption includes the appropriate hashtags and the text included in the captions are relative to the image. There is harmony between the image, video, or GIF and the caption – which is something many brands tend to overlook when uploading content.

They make use of emojis which is a major plus. Social media is all about the emojis, and when they are used appropriately, they can boost the post. Emojis also make the captions livelier.

Their captions, like their posts, are also simple. They do not add unnecessary information or text. Unless it's a dedication or special announcement, Califia Farms' captions are usually short and witty in nature. It takes skill to be able to come up with captions like that. This works for them because followers often respond to the images and the captions.

Their content is relatable. It's clear that Califia Farms has a following that engages in what they upload. Every post has comments underneath them. The comments are often in response to what has been posted.

Califia Farms doesn't upload content that does not relate to their brand or their target audience. They are creative with their advertising

Califia Farms hasn't used their knowledge of their target audience to exploit their interests or overload them with content. The content on Califia Farms' Instagram blog is tailored to connect with followers and first-time viewers on a personal level.

Most of the images are set in locations that are part of people's everyday lives. They place their products on countertops, in supermarkets, at picnics, in workout spaces and on kitchen tables. These are areas that are typical to their target audience. When their followers view their content, they get the impression that the brand understands them and truly cares about their needs. The brand also makes use of young models, who are often kitted out in athletic or casual gear, in their images and videos. This is a reflection of their target audience. When their followers see the models in Califia Farms' posts, they see themselves–they see people they can relate to.

All of this creates a personal connection with their audience. The audience feels like they can depend on the brand because of the care the brand took to make the audience feel represented. When a brand is able to cultivate a following that connects with them and feels loyal to the brand, it is only a matter of time before the brand experiences constant growth.

What Can You Learn from Them?

There is power in simplicity. Often, people make the mistake of thinking that their posts have to have complex designs and a lot of color in order to catch the attention of the audience. Relying on a method like this can actual repel your audience instead of attracting them. When brands focus on unnecessary complications, the structure and nature of the posts are often neglected. For example, if you upload a post with text and a background that is filled with colorful vectors and many brightly-colored streaks, your followers might not be able to decipher the actual message you are trying to pass through the post. Take a look at what is essential for the post, and find simple ways to enhance them. Make use of backgrounds that complement the focal point of your post. Avoid bright colors that can clash with the focal point of your image, unless you are trying to go with a psychedelic theme. You can add accessories to the product if that is what you are trying to capture in order to liven the scene. Position everything in your images, and make sure the image is balanced. Try not to do too much. You may end up missing the mark instead of hitting it. If you are searching for images to use, look for images that are visually balanced. Avoid images that have clashing colors and objects that do not relate to one another.

Know your target audience, and use this knowledge to help you engage with the audience. The mistake many brands make is to gain a full understanding of their audience in order to manipulate them into investing in their brand. Some brands have no care about their target audience, and this always backfires on them. Remember that you are dealing with people who have minds of their own. It is you who needs them. Without the audience, you will have no following, and your blog will be irrelevant. See it as trying to get to know someone better so you can become their friend. Envision your followers as your friends. Engage with them through your captions and through the posts you upload. Make them feel like they are being spoken to and not spoken at. Take their needs and preferences into consideration, and you will win over your target audience with time. Califia Farms' content revolves around their target audience--from the locations they use for their photos, to their captions they write under their images and videos and even to the models they use in their photos. They put great thought into showing their followers and their target audience that they care. And their strategies have yielded great results. That is how important it is to know your target audience. It's one of the major determining factors for the success of your brand. Center your content around your target audience, and you won't go wrong. Create content that will make someone want to respond to it. Take time to plan your content; that's how you will be able to deduce whether it will be engaging and relevant to your target audience.

Tentsile Tree Tents (@tentsile)

Who Are They?

Tentsile Tree Tents is a company that manufactures tents for campers, backpackers and adventurers.

The London-based company caters to a problem many campers experience–rocky ground underneath their tents. To improve the campers' experience, Tentsile Tree Tents manufactured tents that can be set up above the ground. All that is needed are three sturdy trees to attach the ends of the tent. Once off the ground, up to three or four people can be accommodated by the structure. Their outdoor sleeping experience becomes a more comfortable one.

Now, this sounds like a product that has a very particular target audience–campers. The product gives little to work with when it comes to creating aesthetically pleasing images. One wouldn't think that a tent-making company would be interested in advertising on Instagram–an application solely dedicated to imagery. But Tentsile Tree Tents proved many wrong. With a great amount of creativity, the brand has managed to attain over 170,000 followers on Instagram, with the majority of the followership being engaged. That is quite a feat for a company that sells a product many advertisers would write off of marketing. That's quite a feat for any company, really.

But it is a feat the company managed to achieve, and now the company is one of the most sought-after companies when people are interested in purchasing camping gear. The Tentsile Instagram blog is known for its breathtaking images, whilst managing to strategically position their tents in the view. The brand has managed to attract an audience that goes beyond their target audience! People with and without a love for camping visit the blog regularly to view the stunning imagery found on the Instagram blog.

Tentsile has won further brownie points by being a brand that cares about the environment. For every tent bought, the company plants three trees. You can imagine how many trees the company has managed to plant since its growth!

Tentsile managed to take an idea that seemed to be 'too specific,' and they proved their critics and naysayers wrong. They created a global experience out of their idea. They went on to further take their marketing strategy to a global scale. One would have expected the blog to only attract followers who would be interested in the concept of camping. But they've managed to build their brand around people's love for travel and beautiful sights. They expanded their target audience by appealing to a desire many people have– the desire to travel and experience breathtaking scenery. They managed to cover two parts of the Travel niche–camping and sightseeing. It takes great skill, planning and thinking to be able to achieve such success. This a brand many can learn from. They've managed to take challenges that would often hinder the success of other brands, and they made it work in their favor. As they showcase different sights, with their tents positioned in the shots, they are managing to inspire campers and people who have never camped before to purchase their products and experience the sights they find on Tentsile's Instagram blog.

Chapter 6. Branding, Selling & Buying Accounts

Branding Instagram Accounts

The main aim of branding is to create an emotional connection between a business and its consumers. This is achieved through a combination of several marketing elements such as brand name, colors, logos and more. Branding enables a business to differentiate itself in a crowded market. On Instagram, it is possible to brand your business through visuals (visual branding). A strong Instagram branding is key to achieving success in marketing your business through Instagram. The thing with branding your account is that you should ensure that your overall business branding matches perfectly with the content you would want the target audience to view. For instance, if your brand employs lots of bright colors, so should your uploaded content. Here are some tips for branding your account.

Always Upload Beautiful Content

Beautiful content is the key to branding as it draws the attention of users to your brand. Your target audience will have first-hand experience with your visual representation and this will determine whether they will follow your account or even inquire about your brand, therefore, your content must be great. If you are unable to take high-quality photos of your brand, there are lots of copyright-free images where you can find beautiful high-quality photos. Additionally, you should ensure uploaded photos are clear, have high contrast and are well lit. You can also try uploading photos coupled with text to catch the attention of your audience and tell a story using visual items.

Uniformed Instagram Appearance

It may be challenging to take astonishing photos and upload them on a constant basis, but consistency is vital for visual branding. Strategize on the appearance of your Instagram account, whether you would want your brand to be vintage, classy, romantic or dramatic, always be consistent. You can use Instagram filters to enhance your images and get the emotional attention of your audience. Instagram filters such as Juno, Lark, and Clarendon increases the contrast of your posts while Reyes, Crema and Gingham make photos appear more pale and subdued. Photoshop software can also be used to achieve the best results for uniformity of your posts.

Tag your Post with Unique Hashtags.

Additionally, hashtags elicit engagements among your audience, marketing your brand in the process. You should use at least two hashtags per post that are unique to your brands such as the name of your business or brand name. Unique hashtags are a simple way to increase the familiarity of your audience with your brand and is vital especially in branding a newly opened business.

Buying and Selling Instagram Accounts

Just like domain names and websites, Instagram accounts can be traded, although it is against their terms of services. As per Instagram terms of services, you are restricted to "sell, license, transfer or assign your accounts, followers, usernames and other account rights to any other user." Therefore, an authentic way buy accounts is not available and you should be careful when buying accounts as they are mostly filled with scammers. However, if you wish to buy an Instagram account for your business, there are available forums where Instagram accounts are advertised, and you can contact a broker to buy the account. Again, be very careful when buying accounts from these forums as they clearly state that buying accounts is at your own risk

The other option in buying accounts is to explore accounts advertising themselves for sale on Instagram. Instagram accounts can advertise themselves for sale just like domain names and you can contact the account owner through a DM or an email that is usually provided in the bio. It is important to close the transaction face to face to avoid being defrauded of your hard-earned cash.

eBay also offers a platform where you can buy Instagram accounts and is a safer platform. However, recently eBay has stopped advertising accounts for sale on their platform as it is against Instagram terms of services and could lead to hefty fines.

There are also account selling sites such as Viral Instas and Fameswap where you could buy accounts from. From reviews, these platforms seem legit and you can safely buy accounts from them. They also come with a hashtag research app containing more than five hundred hashtags related to each page and the contents best suited for an account based on the followers or audience.

Selling an Instagram account may be challenging given by the fact that is against Instagram terms of services. However, it depends on the niche. For instance, if your account is based on hotel niche and your followers are food lovers, you can approach a hotel online and sell your account to them. You can also advertise on your account bio such as "Account for sale, contact: sale@email.com."

Instagram account buyers mostly look for the following things before buying an account

• *Account name – Instagram accounts with shorter names are preferred by account buyers and are worth more, especially a "brandable" username. Copyright accounts pretending to be a celebrity account or accounts with long names are usually shunned by new buyers.*

• *Account engagement – Accounts with not only many followers but also their engagement such as liking and commenting on a post are preferred by most buyers as they are sure of continuous growth and even worth more compared to inactive accounts*

• Account Niche – Account niche defines the types of your followers and is an important factor in determining the price of an account. Common account types that deal with memes, funny videos, vines and other content are worth less and may not be effective in marketing your brand. Accounts dealing in products such as cars, gadgets, fashion, fitness and other content of the same nature are worth more and can easily market your brand.

It is hard to determine the real worth of an account looking at statistics or insights, but the general rule should be 0.50-3.00USD per a thousand followers based in Europe, Australia, Canada and North America. Remember always sell your account in secret away from the public eyes as Instagram can suspend any account they establish has been sold. Be careful not to give out your account login details before being handed the payment, as you can easily be swindled.

Chapter 7. How to Market the Brand and Increase Sales

While there are many people that will get an Instagram account in order to show some of their own personal things and their day to day life online, you can also use this social media site in order to show off your business and as part of the marketing campaign. There are a lot of things that Instagram will be able to do to help out your business, including to help your brand get out to more people, helping you to get more followers, and helping you to find some good paying customers.

According to some online marketers, Instagram has already surpassed Twitters in terms of how many users are on the social media site each month. This means that you will be able to get your account set up on Instagram and engage with your customers, knowing that they are more likely to come back than on other social media sites.

Create a separate account for the business

If you are looking to use Instagram for your business, you need to make sure that it is not mixed with your personal account if you have one. This can confuse your customers if you do try to make your personal and business account into one. You need to make sure that there is an account that is just for your business and that will make the company look great.

In this section, make sure that you are not focusing on yourself. Your personal site can be great for pictures of vacations and all the fun things that you get to do, but there is no place for this on your business Instagram page. It is best to leave these pictures and thoughts for that personal account and focus instead on things that relate to your business on this new page.

In order to make sure that your business account is as effective as possible, here are a few things that you should try out:

• Be consistent with the profile picture and your name. You need to have relevance and consistency when it comes to using this as a marketing tool and you shouldn't be able to confuse the fans by what is there. This is why using the same name and picture on all of your social media platforms can help to avoid confusion.

• Make sure that you have information about your website somewhere on the page. The bio is going to be really great for putting this in because Instagram can be strict about this and the bio is about the only place that this will work on Instagram. While you are at it, make sure that the bio is informative and catches the attention of your fans.

• Inside the bio, make sure to list the name of your business at least a few times. Don't let the bio get too long, but make it light and catchy without a lot of sales talk inside of it.

Share the content that others want to see

For the most part, your users would rather use pictures rather than written words. Even some of the simplest pictures can be effective at spreading your message quickly. And Instagram is really focused on images so it is a good idea to use these. Instagram doesn't usually allow for a lot of long articles and blog type materials because it would rather that you post videos or photos and this is going to work out great when you are working on your marketing campaign.

Many shoppers like to use Instagram because it does focus so much on pictures. This makes it easier for them to take a look at the products that they are interested in and even compare it to some of the other offerings that are on the market. They don't want to read a long blog about the item; they would rather get a chance to see good pictures of the product so make sure that a good deal of your page will focus on these pictures and videos.

Another thing that you should work on is avoiding the hard sell. Most buyers that are on social networking sites are there to collect some information before they make the sale. Many of these are going to be influenced by the activities that are on the social media of the business. If this is good, you will get more sales but if it is bad, you will lose them. Using pushy captions on your pictures is not going to work. Just focus on sharing some great pictures of what you have to offer and spend the captions describing the item. Never force the audience, just give them the information that they need to make the purchase.

There are also a few editing tools that are built into Instagram and can be great for helping you to make your pictures stand out. there are millions of these photos that are added to the platform all of the time and this makes it hard to fight against the competition. You can use some of these filters in order to make the images look better so that they begin to stand out.

Some businesses like to offer some promos to their Instagram followers. There was recently a study done that showed how 41 percent of users on Instagram were willing to follow a business in order to get the promotions and giveaways, even if they hadn't purchased from the business in the past, making it a good incentive to offer these to your followers. Try to make it something fun and make sure that your followers know that this is an exclusive deal just for some of your Instagram followers.

Reach more of your audience

While uploading some good photos is a good way to reach some of your audience and can make it easier to get the results that you want, you also need to do a bit work and have a plan for others to view the photos and follow your page there are many things that you will be able to do to make this happen.

First, hashtags are going t be great because they make it easier for others to see your photos. Most of your fans are gong to see that their feeds are quickly changing so it is easy for the pictures may get buried down before the followers are able to see them when they are away. Using hashtags is going to increase the lifespan of these posts. It is so effective that at least 88 percent of posts on Instagram are going to have at least one hashtag. Of course, you should be careful when picking out the one that you would like to use, picking options that relate to the business and the product, and make sure that you aren't using them excessively.

Look for some brand ambassadors

Forming up a group of ambassadors who are able to share information about your brand with some other users is a great way to reach more people. You can ask some of your followers to share their reviews and their pictures so that you increase your exposures. In some recent surveys, you will find that 78 percent of buyers are going to make their purchases based on the brand and the presence that it has on social media. Thus, when you ask your followers to praise the services and products that you have for sale, it can lead you to some more.

The process for finding these ambassadors can be simple. You will need to find some good hashtags for all of your marketing campaign, encourage other customers and followers to post their own photos and reviews as they relate to your brand. And then when you find out which people are doing this, make sure to reward them in some manner, whether it is through shout outs, discounts, or freebies of some sort.

Encourage interaction with the content

If you want to increase your presence online, you need to make sure that your followers are engaged. Inside of Instagram, you are going to get about 331 engagements if there are around 10,000 followers who are willing to share a photo. This is much higher than some of the other social media sites, but there are some other things that you can do to increase this number including:

Write out some active captions. This can include a call to action, a question, or information about the product if you would like.

Hold a contest: this will help to increase your engagement because people will want to get in on the rewards and they will feel valuable. Make sure to pick out the prize ahead of time and find a way to encourage people to follow. For example, you can choose to have people like some of the pictures that you have to get entered into the contest.

Respond to your followers: if your followers are asking questions online and you never respond, you will find that it is difficult to keep them around. You need to reply to their comments, answer their questions, follow them, or thank them to make them feel valuable.

Measure how successful the Instagram campaign

As you are working on your campaign, you will want to make sure that you are taking care to track how the campaign is going. If you just throw a few things out online and you don't keep track of the campaign, you will find that things could be going horribly wrong and you have no idea. Placing some measurements in place can help you see how the campaign is doing and make changes if something doesn't seem to be going right.

Make sure that you create a few checkpoints throughout your campaign to help you to check up on things. You can always experiment with something new as well, but make sure that you check out the measurements to see if this is actually successful for you or not. As a new business, you never know what is going to work for you and what isn't going to work so take the time to try out a few things and see what works. Over time, you will be able to see some great results and can stick with the things that work.

Marketing your brand on Instagram can be really successful especially when it is compared to some of the other social media sites, but you need to make sure that you are doing it the proper way so that you bring out the customers and the followers that you would like. Follow some of these steps and you are all set to go with a great marketing campaign.

Chapter 8. Instagram Ad Campaigns

Successfully creating and launching an ad campaign on Instagram might sound a little scary. It is quite easy if you know what you need to do.

Step One: Research

The first step is to find the inspiration for your Instagram ads by analyzing the things that others in your niche or your industry are doing. Before you create an ad campaign, you need to check what your competitors are doing. You need to spend some time researching the kind of ads they are running, the call-to-actions they use, and the engagement they are able to get.

One of the easiest ways to do this research is to view your competitor's Instagram handle and go through their mobile website. Now, you need to go through their product page and check the specific products. If that specific Instagram account uses Facebook pixel for remarketing, then once you return to your Instagram page, you will start to see their ads on your feed along with the products you searched for. If you repeat these steps with different competitors, it will give you an idea about the type of ads they are running. Also, it is a great way to find some inspiration and ideas to design your own campaign.

Step Two: Campaign Objective

Before we delve into how Instagram ad works, you will need to establish a campaign objective. A campaign objective states the purpose the ads serve, and it essentially dictates what you want viewers to do when they see your ads on Instagram. There are different campaign objectives that Instagram offers, and it is given in the form of a pre-made list. The objective that you choose from this list helps optimize the ads and determines how you pay for the same. For instance, if your aim is to gain more followers, then the click-through on the ads will not be your primary priority. The different campaign objectives that you can choose on Instagram are as follows:

Brand awareness helps you reach the audience who are likely to pay attention to your ads and increases the overall awareness of your business.

Reach - Select this objective to increase the reach of your ads.

Traffic - It is ideal to opt for this objective to increase the drive the traffic to your website or the app store (if you have an app).

App installs - Directing traffic to the app store so that they can install or purchase your app.

Engagement – Engagement is important to increase the number of people who see and engage with your page or posts. It includes comments, shares, likes and, responses you receive.

Video views - As the name suggests, it is to promote the number of views the videos you post garner.

Conversion - To convert your audience into paying customers or to make any other similar valuable action.

If your marketing objective is to sell products or to run a remarketing campaign, then it is a good idea to install Facebook pixel. It is a small code that you can place on your business website to track the visitors and any other conversions. When you use Facebook pixel, whenever someone clicks on the Instagram ad, they visit the website and make a purchase, and the pixel shows a conversion. Then this conversion is matched against all those who click on your Instagram ad to see the sales or conversions you have made with a specific ad.

Step Three: Targeting

Instagram ad targeting helps you find the best audience to whom you can advertise a specific ad to. For instance, if your business sells quirky socks, you will obviously want to target all those people who are likely to make a purchase. It's a great thing that Instagram ads have similar targeting options Facebook ads. You have different targeting options like location, demographics, behavior, interests, and much more.

At the primary level, your campaign needs a specific geographical region (country), gender (if it is a gender-specific product or service) and ideal age group. For instance, you can have a campaign that targets men and women between the ages of 18 to 40 who live in metropolitan cities. Try to be as specific with this as possible while you are targeting your audience. The greater the reach of the targeting ads, the better your chances of attaining conversions or obtaining your campaign goal.

Instagram also offers the option of creating custom audiences to reach all those who have interacted with your business in the past or with similar businesses.

Step Four: Creative

The fourth step is to build your Instagram ads creative. This is partially a science and an art in itself. Before you start, you need to think about your objective, the audience you are reaching and the kind of message you must deliver to encourage your audience to engage with the ad. Instagram offers different types of ad formats to choose from and they are photo, carousel, slideshow, and video ads.

Photo ads

You can use these ads to tell the story of your brand and feature different products by using visual imagery that's engaging. If you are just getting started with using ads on Instagram, then this is the safest and the easiest option to start with. Not only are they easy to set up but are easy to run as well.

Carousel ads

If you want to strategically showcase various products or multiple uses of a given product, then opt for this ad format. This format of ad allows the user to swipe to see more images and includes a call-to-action button that will direct them to a landing page to learn more. For instance, a restaurant can use this type of ads to showcase all the different ingredients used to prepare a tasty meal. Once the viewer swipes through all the images, you can use a call-to-action button that will direct users to a reservation page or something similar.

Video ads

A video ad can last for up to 60 seconds. Ensure that your ad is great and that you use the first 30 seconds wisely. This is the time frame within which users will want to engage with the business. When you are designing these ads, you need to create content that integrates well into your follower's feed.

Slideshow ads

You can create a simple video ad using a series of stills. This is a good type of ad, if you don't want to spend a lot of time creating video content for your business.

Businesses also tend to use user-generated content. If you want to promote a product using ads on Instagram, try to include some real-life situations or testimonials that your audience can relate to.

Step Six: Tracking

You will need to edit and constantly optimize your ad campaign on Instagram to generate the best results. There are different tools that you can use to track the performance of your ads on Instagram. The tools that you use will depend on the size of your business and the number of ads you wish to run. Use Power Editor if you want to manage multiple campaigns or if you want precise control over the advertising campaigns. If you are part of a large business team, then use Facebook's Ad Manager. If you are just starting out with Instagram marketing, then use Ads Manager.

Step Six: Tools to Use

The list of social media tools that you can make use of is endless; you might need some help to figure out the best options that are available. Following are some of the most helpful social media tools:

Mention - This can be thought of as the Google alerts for social media. Mention is considered one of the best tools that can help you monitor the presence of your brand on the World Wide Web. Mention also has certain features that let you respond to the mentions that have been made to your brand and to share the news that you might have come across with the industry.

Buffer - This is a really powerful analytical tool that integrates social media publishing in it. Buffer is a helpful social media tool that helps send your updates to the giants of social networking platforms such as LinkedIn, Instagram, Facebook, Twitter, Google+, and App.net. This tool comes with an analytic system that is inbuilt and lets you understand the reason why particular posts tend to be working better than the other posts and also the best possible time for making any particular publication based upon the requirements of your audience. Not just this, it also lets you collaborate with your team and keep the account updated with fresh content regularly.

Feedly- Feedly is a content discovery tool. You won't just find good content, you can also share your findings with your audience without trouble. You get to subscribe to the RSS feeds to help keep in tune with all the recent updates on the industry blogs as well as news sites. If you are interested in a topic, then Feedly can be made use of for tracking related content.

Zapier - This is a platform that acts as a connector for all the various services that you make use of individually and lets you synchronize them all to make your work simpler. For instance, if your team usually makes use of HipChat for keeping in touch then by making use of Zapier you will be able to set up the option for automatic notifications within HipChat rooms for any new updates. You will be able to connect all the various apps that you are making use of. If all your apps are integrated on a common platform then your work gets much simpler.

Bottlenose - Bottlenose now comes with a new feature that has a real-time search engine that consolidates all the information from social networking sites and various groups and displays the resultant information in an order or algorithmic importance. The result of all this work is a stream of content that has already been marked from most to least important. When you have information that is already arranged according to your needs, your work gets simpler. You can also share any of the search results. You can also integrate Buffer and Bottlenose for adding any additional content and resources that can be utilized on a later date, if you don't want to overwhelm your followers.

Quintly - This is a really powerful tool that can be made use of for obtaining detailed analytics of social media and helps you keep a track of your business on social media platforms such as Facebook, Twitter, YouTube, Google+, LinkedIn and Instagram as well. Quintly also helps you to benchmark those features that help you compare your performance with those of your competitors in the industry and also against the industry averages. The Quintly dashboard also provides for customization so that you can simply focus on the stats that matter more to you when compared to the rest.

Use these different apps to track your performance on Instagram.

Chapter 9. Sell Your Own Photos

Instagram was created to be an image-sharing platform and, in spite of its many new features, its primary purpose remains unchanged: sharing photos with your friends across the globe. However, as a smart and cunning online entrepreneur you will recognize that photos are also **assets**. Photos can be branded, licensed and *sold* in many different ways and on a wide range of online marketplaces.

I have worked with many Instagram creators who are outstanding photographers and graphic designers; by selling their own photography and designs they have developed monthly incomes as high as $12,000.

Due to a tremendous lack in the skill, I have never used this approach myself. However, it can be a very straightforward high-earning opportunity if you are an excellent photographer or graphic designer. For this reason, I will still describe how YOU can make thousands of dollars each month selling Instagram photos or graphic designs in the following chapter.

Many artists sell direct copies of their Instagram posts, known as **Instagram prints.** For popular Instagram pages built on high-quality photography, I have seen prints easily sell in the range of $40-150. Other artists use Instagram to showcase some of their work and funnel followers to an online destination where they can purchase photography or designs directly.

How can you prevent people from stealing your photography?

If you showcase your photography on Instagram in high-resolution, people can visualize your photo and take a screenshot to obtain a free copy. Of course, if you have licensed your photo you can sue them for theft and unauthorized use of your proprietary content. However, this is extremely expensive and time-consuming path.

The most common option is to showcase a low-resolution version of your photos on Instagram with a custom watermark filter that uniquely identifies the images as your property. If they wish to obtain a full-quality image without any form of branding they must purchase a copy from your website.

How to add custom watermark?

The following tools are extremely convenient to add custom watermarks/branding in your photos:

-       *Adobe Photoshop*: most serious photographers have experience working with Adobe Photoshop. If you are a regular user, you will know just how easy it is to create and add a unique watermark to all your photos

-       *WinWatermark.com* – this is a tool that was especially developed to easily create and implement unique watermarks. This tool comes in both free and paid-for versions.

www.Digimarc.com

This website offers unique image-tracking software that adds invisible watermarks to your photos; these allow you to identify any internet location where your image is displayed.

The main advantage of this platform is the invisible watermark. The main drawback is that it only points out where this image is being displayed without your authorization. Afterwards it is up to you to pursue a refund, which can be extremely difficult. Furthermore, not having a watermark often represents an incentive to steal your image instead of making a purchase. The yearly cost of this software is 50$, so you might wish to further research its features before purchasing.

Where can you sell your photos?

If you wish to sell your photos/designs online there are two main options for you to consider (1) online marketplace and (2) personal website.

Online Marketplace

There are many well-established online marketplaces where artists such as photographers and graphic designers can sell their work. These are websites where thousands of artists share their work, advertise it and offer it for purchase.

Advantages:

-       Easy to set up your own profile and place photos for sale

-       Marketplace already has customers

Disadvantages:

-        You do not have full control of the style/portfolio/bio displayed

-        You must pay a commission to the website

-        Typically your work will find a lower price point on these marketplaces due to high competition

Recommended Options: These are the most popular marketplaces where artists can easily showcase and sell their photography/designs. I suggest visiting each of these websites and explore their offers to fully evaluate how they can help you sell your work

-        500px.com
-        **Twenty20.com**

Your Personal Online Shop

Creating your online shop is a popular choice to sell photography and custom designs; most professional and high-earning artists follow this path. This choice is definitely more complex than a marketplace, but if done correctly a well-designed website can greatly boost your sales.

Advantages:

-        You can control every aspect of the website: contact links, portfolio, BIO, etc...

-        The professional look and lesser competition typically means your work will sell for a higher price range

-        -You do not have to pay any commissions

Disadvantages:

-        Website can be difficult and expensive to create

•   You can hire some excellent web developers at upwork.com

•   To create a website yourself, wordpress.com is the most popular choice

-        You are responsible for 100% of your website visitors. You must have well-established following on Instagram or your website will not receive any traffic

Recommended Options:

-        **Shopify.com** – as explained earlier this is the most popular online platform to create your own personal online store. It contains well-established apps that allow customers to easily make purchases and pay directly into your bank account

-    **Wordpress.com** – this is another very popular online platform that allows you to build your own website. This platform is free and is very well-known for its vast range of ready-made themes and templates available. You are not limited to creating an online store, but can build any type of website on this platform. If you are planning to build extensive portfolios and informational pages about yourself as a photographer/designer this may be a more appropriate choice.

Become Active on Multiple Social Media

Brands pay you depending on the total number of people you can influence, full stop.

On Instagram this is quantified using two parameters: total number of followers and audience engagement. If you wish to increase your Instagram income in a long-term fashion, your only choice is to increase one of the two above parameters.

A second option is to increase your reach as an influencer by diversifying your content distribution platforms beyond Instagram. Most influencers are active on multiple platforms to include Facebook,

Twitter and YouTube; together these platforms report *billions* of monthly active users.

Becoming active on multiple platforms has a powerful synergistic effect, i.e. most of your Instagram are redirected to your YouTube account and your YouTube subscribers are redirected to your Instagram page.

It is critical you become active on multiple social media platforms to increase your total audience reach and thus receive significantly higher salaries in return.

It can be difficult to get started correctly on other social media platforms and YouTube if you only have Instagram experience. Each platform has its tricks and you must approach them correctly or you can severely damage your reputation.

Chapter 10. Instagram DM Groups

Instagram DM groups, also referred to as Instagram engagement groups, are used by Instagram users to engage among themselves through:

- *Commenting and liking each other's post*
- *Viewing each other's Stories*
- Commenting or replying to each other's Story timeline

Basically, Instagram engagement groups are aimed at driving more comments, likes, and followers to accounts in the group thereby steadily growing them. Most Instagram DM groups are created on Instagram with others found on Facebook, Telegram, WhatsApp and other social media platforms. Depending on the engagement group.

How do Instagram DM Groups work?

Instagram engagement groups work in a very simple way referred to as "like for like" strategy. Instagram accounts with almost the same number of followers are pooled together in a group either on Instagram,

Telegram, Facebook, and other forums. On joining such groups, you are obliged to engage in all videos and photos uploaded by members of the group to their Instagram accounts by liking, commenting, and tagging your followers or other Instagram users. In return, your account will be engaged with other similar accounts through likes, comments, and tags leading to spectacular growth through or following.

Joining Instagram DM Groups

Instagram DM groups are closed groups operating in secret. Therefore, it may be challenging to find and join a group. However, you can join these groups by sending a direct request (DM) to the group owner or a member of a group you would like to join. Usually, Instagram DM groups have different rules for enrolling new members. Some would charge you a small fee for joining while others are free and would require your active participation in liking and commenting on all photos or videos posted within the group. To locate these groups, you can use search engines, notably Google, as some are found on online forums or blogs of Instagram influencers. It is worth noting that Instagram engagement groups take time to grow your account, therefore you must be patient and dedicated to achieving success.

DM Groups on Instagram

These are the most common types of engagement groups and are usually found on Instagram. When a member uploads a new post to their Instagram account, he/she notifies the group members through a DM. Each group member must then engage in the published post by liking or commenting on the post as soon as possible. Similarly, before you can post, you must have engaged other members' posts. The comments and likes gained from group members assist in enhancing engagement and visibility of your account on Instagram, which is vital in gaining new followers.

Instagram Groups on Telegram

Instagram groups on Telegram operate correspondingly to DM groups, however, they have several key differences. First, they are hosted on Telegram and have thousands of members. The group is structured in a way that members can publish posts at specific time "rounds" rather than post sporadically throughout the day. This is to ensure that every post gets maximum engagement from the group members, thereby you are assured of account growth. Additionally, you get to choose which time "round" when you are most active on Instagram to post and you are not indebted to recover a period you missed posting or you did not participate in the group.

PRO TIP: Choose Telegram Engagement Group over Instagram DM Groups.

Telegram Engagement groups are much more effective in growing your account compared to Instagram DM groups. The Instagram algorithm "pleased" when a post gets more engagements at a faster rate, which can easily be achieved through Telegram engagement groups and may not be the case with Instagram DM groups since your post gains likes and comments intermittently rather than once. Also, Instagram DM groups are restricted to 15 people per group, thereby it may not be effective in generating enough engagements to grow your account. With a high engagement rate, your account will be featured on the Explore Page where it will be displayed to a much wider audience who may end up following you.

Chapter 11. How to Hold an Instagram Contest

This contest concept has shown positive results for nearly any business on Instagram, as it generates lots of customer interest. It is a quick and effective way to engage customers on your account and get even more followers who get excited about the subsequent rewards you offer.

The best part is there are quite a few simple, yet amazing types of contests you can hold on your Instagram account. Read on to get a better idea of each.

Types of Instagram contests:

• One simple and random type of contest is where you ask your users to follow and like a particular post. You can randomly choose a winner from amongst all the users who do so. Give a deadline until the contest is valid and announce the winner after that. The prize you offer can be your own product and if they like the prize, you have a returning customer for sure. This type of contest is a very simple way to gain more likes and followers at the same time.

- Another type of contest is where the users have to post a particular type of picture and use a specific hashtag relevant to your contest. The theme could be anything from asking users to post a picture of him or her or wearing something like a pink dress. The user needs to upload the picture and tag your Instagram account. They also need to use the specific hashtag that you create for your contest. The next part is that the winner with the best picture and maximum number of likes on their post will be the winner. You can then choose the winner after the contest deadline passes and announce the result on your page along with what you will be gifting the winner. It's a simple and effective concept where the pictures are easy-to-take selfies. Most customers find such contests appealing and will participate every time you hold such events, for the simple reason it's easy and they just might win.

- Yet another concept for those with an actual offline business is an in-store photo contest. This works for brands or shops that have an Instagram account and an actual setup customers can walk into. Your contest rules ask them to click pictures in your actual store and then upload the picture on Instagram. They have to tag your account and use the relevant hashtag. This allows you to attract more customers into your store via foot traffic, as well as engage them online. The contest timeline can be range from a week to a month. A weekly period gives a faster call to action and results.

• You can also allow contest participants to enter through your website as well as Instagram. Giving more options means you get more people who might or might not be using other platforms. Just make it clear they can use the option of Instagram or the company website.

• Yet another type of photo contest is where the customer is required to upload a picture with your products. The post needs to show how they use your products and also include a contest-specific hashtag. This way, other people get to see more real people actually using your product. A lot of potential customers can be generated this way. The users will also make a personal effort of making the images appealing to their own followers as well as to those judging the contest. It is also very brand-related and is a good marketing strategy. You can then offer up your products to these participants for their loyalty value. One example of this is be if you are a makeup company. Ask the users to create a particular look with your products and show what they have used clearly in their entry. It's amazing to see how many people get interested in such a contest and might use this as an excuse to go ahead to buy new things in order to participates.

As you can see, there are a lot of easy and creative ways to utilize Instagram contests to your benefit. Everybody loves free gifts, so entering a simple and fun Instagram contest is quite appealing to most people. While you part with some simple stuff you already have, you generate much more traffic that will pay to get the same stuff. Users don't have to spend a penny to enter the contest and you earn more than tenfold of the one penny you part with. So go ahead and try holding a contest from your account. The results are more than likely to be positive.

Use the following tips to hold a successful contest on your Instagram account:

☐ First, set a proper goal or objective you want to meet with your contest. Everything you do needs to have a purpose and positive result.

☐ Now, think clearly about the target customers you want to reach through your contest. Your contest specifications will depend according to whom you want as your participant or future customer.

☐ Depending on what your goal and target market is, decide what you will be giving away as a prize. It should be something that will make your followers and other users want to take part in the contest. The prize should also be decided upon depending on a budget that you should not cross. Just make sure that the incentive is such that it engages your target crowd.

☐ The post you put up to announce your contest should also be appealing and attention grabbing. You can also show the customers the prize they will be getting if they win. Make it as attractive as possible.

☐   According to the target customers whom you want to reach, decide on what type of contest you are holding. You already know there are different types of contests you can hold and modify them creatively. For instance, if your brand sells tea, ask users to upload selfies of themselves drinking from your particular brand of tea. Similarly, decide on a particular unique theme for your contest.

☐   Manage the contest by asking all the participants to use a specific hashtag you create for your contest. They should also tag your account in the post so you can keep track of all the entries. Make sure you set specific rules for any entries so only users who follow these will be eligible to participate in the contest. One of the basics is that they actually follow your Instagram account.

☐   The hashtag for the contest is actually quite important. It should not be something people commonly use. That would make it difficult to determine who is actually entering your contest. The unique contest hash tag makes a community just for your participants so they can view each other's entries easily.

☐   Set a deadline for when the contest is running and until when entries will be accepted. Small weekly contests have been found to be quite engaging and productive. It keeps generating traffic and the investment does not have to be over the top either. If your prize is much bigger however, you can allow a longer deadline to make the users actually work for it. In case of such big prizes, you might choose to have terms such as the picture with the maximum likes wins the contest. This gives the participants more time to work towards the likes and allows more users to view your brand name as well. Make sure you also clearly mention on what basis you will be choosing the winners of the contest in order to avoid any confusion or conflict.

☐ Depending on the results you see from your contest, determine how often you want to hold them. If you see good and quick results with a lot more new customers, it makes it feasible to have frequent contests. Otherwise, take it a little slower with a monthly or seasonal contest.

☐ To get more participants for your contest, promote it in as many forums as possible. Announce the contest on your website or any other social media in which you have a presence. This could be anything from Facebook, Twitter, a blog you have, etc. You can also make other popular account holders on Instagram announce the contest on their personal account. You can also use ads on Facebook or Twitter and other such places that will allow more people to see what's being offered.

☐ Once your contests are up and running, monitor it closely. Use tools like Google analytics, Google alerts, Twitter analytics, or other such third party options. These will help you easily and effectively monitor your contest until it ends.

☐   All you have to do when you choose the winner is contact them and announce it on your page. You can take it a step further by uploading a great picture of the winner with the actual prize that you sent them. These makes more users interested and looking forward to the next contest that you will be holding.

Chapter 12. Instagram Page Vs Facebook Fan Page

Instagram and Facebook business page are both great and must have for our business. The major difference between Instagram page and Facebook business page is that with Instagram we can get free traffic while with Facebook free traffic is not always guarantee. We need both of this platform to run a successful business because both platforms is a great platform and almost all our audiences are already on this platform and that is the major reason everybody must consider utilizing this two platform to skyrocket their businesses.

Facebook Business Page

Having Facebook business page for your business is a must because with that you can always gather similar people who are interested in a specific niche in one place and reach out to them anytime you want. But what happens mostly is that Facebook limits their reach. Meaning when you make a post on your fan page, your post will only have the opportunity to reach a few number people.

Another thing with Facebook is that people are not actively searching for an interest (niche). This is because Facebook major purpose so to connect friend and family together and also suggest post to you based on who your friend is, things you like and what you are doing on their platform which is why Facebook marketing is very important for business owner because Facebook collect everything you do on their website and they also know 70% to 90% about you. To proof, this, assume you basketball lover and you have like various fan pages about basket ball and add most basket ball lover as a friend. Now you scroll through your Facebook news feed and see post your friend (basketball lover) post on Facebook. Your comment, like and share that post to your own timeline.

The secret behind this is that Facebook now knows that you are basket ball lover because you engaged mostly on their platform on basketball content.

Now a business owner who doesn't know (not your friend on FB) you set up a fan page related to basket ball (maybe selling the item) and run a promotion on Facebook targeting basket ball. Because you have interacted much on basketball on Facebook then

Facebook will suggest that post to you via news feed and if you interested, you may or may not purchase.

This is because Facebook store your data and they know what you like and dislike. Also, that is what make paid ads work well on Facebook.

Instagram Business Page

Instagram is a little more different from Facebook because of the ability to reach more people even without you spending money on ads. It is easy to grow Instagram page fast than grow a Facebook fan page.

If you can invest more time in growing an Instagram page you can get thousands of follower fast because there is no limit in reaching people.

The cool thing about Instagram and why Instagram is much better than Facebook is that people are actively searching for your niches by entering their keyword (#dog or dog) in the search box. If you have done what is expected to be done and your content appears on the discovery feed, you can reach thousands and millions of people in less than 30 minute. All this happen because Instagram does not limit your reach, you are the only one that can limit your reach if you are too lazy in growing your Instagram page.

Another cool thing about Instagram is that people are always engaged with your content than Facebook content because Facebook limit their reach and they want to spend money on ads

Let me ask you this

Have you ever see a Facebook fan page with 1million fans but when you check their engagement, they hardly get 50 like and comment

Also, check Instagram page with 100k follower, and see what their engagement is

If I am to ask you again, which of this page do you think will be more profitable?

Is it the one with 1M Facebook fan page but less engagement or the one with 100k follower with a thousand plus engagement?

Now you get the idea of how this work.

Furthermore, with Instagram you get free traffic and follower because people are searching for your niche but with Facebook, you can pay to get traffic even pay to buy fans and likes to your fan page

Custom Audience With Instagram

If you are getting a boat load of engagement on your Instagram page and you have Shopify e-commerce store. When you promote your product to your page, you will get a lot of visitor to your website and those visitors may add the product to cart or purchase an item from your store. Once that happens, we can take those data to Facebook to build a similar audience of our website visitor.

In general sense, Instagram help in building a custom audience that can be used for advance Facebook marketing even without no Facebook pixel installed on the Shopify e-commerce store.

Now, we can now see that both Instagram and Facebook work together in growing a business online fast and which one you should start using if you are brand new to online marketing and doesn't have more money to spend on ads.

Driving Revenue With Instagram

Let's focus on what we're all here for. Driving revenue with Instagram.

It's something that turns many potential brands off the platform. It's a blessing in disguise. The absence of links across most of the app makes it more difficult for spam to show up in your feed.

Your ask almost always involves people going to your bio and clicking on the link. The problem is people don't like to go to the bio because it's either poorly created or nonexistent. You won't have that problem.

The important part is your caption. Make the most of it by adding a call to action to click the link in your bio and add a short memorable URL. The link should be trackable and take them to a specific page so you can keep an eye on traffic, conversions, and revenue from Instagram.

Asking isn't enough. Sending them to a sales page isn't enough. You have to reward people for clicking through to your page. Give them something of value. Something you know they'd want before finally asking for a sale.

In an ideal situation, you'll get an email address in exchange for what you give them. Use that contact information to market to them until they decide to unsubscribe. You can easily do this without straying from the tone and imagery of your IG account.

How?

Because you created an IG page that reflects your brand, not the other way around. The key to your Instagram promotion is to use it sparingly. An ad that exclusively asks people to click the link in your bio should only appear at least every 10th post.

The rest is pure value content.

Of course, your page will be a major driver of traffic and revenue from Instagram. It doesn't and shouldn't be the only method you use. There are many other ways such as Instagram ads and Influencers.

I want to focus on Influencers because they've proven time and time again that they can drive engagement, brand awareness, and revenue.

Influencers

An influencer is an individual or group of individuals who sway public opinion. This can be for or against a cause. With the rise of social media, ordinary people are able to wield massive influence that directly translates to revenue for brands.

Whether you want to be an influencer or not, the established players in your field can help you accomplish your aim. Let's look at how to use influencers to grow your following and drive direct revenue.

How to find them
Influencers aren't hard to find. They're the people that end up on your discover page over and over again. The hard part is discovering niche influencers.

Not all influencers will be as effective for your business.

Let's say there's a page that caters to pug lovers. You sell shirts, mugs, posters, and everything in between. The first instinct of many Instagram users is to find a huge account that focuses on pets.

Can you see the problem with this approach?

An account that focuses on pets will also have content related to cats, parrots, hamsters, and anything else people keep as pets. The majority of the people following the page aren't interested in pugs.

When an ad the pug store owner posts on the pet page does poorly, she decides to try a page specific for dogs. They're on the right track now. But dogs is also a large niche. You have Golden Retrievers, German shepherds, Collies, Bull Mastiffs, and Pugs.

The page owner tries her luck and actually makes a few sales. It doesn't cover her expenses but she's encouraged. She decided to tweak the imagery, copy, and call to action on her sponsored post. She's tries again and again. She's making sales, but it's not covering the amount she's spending to advertise and still turn a profit.

She decides Instagram marketing isn't for her and puts it on the backburner. In reality, she was almost there. If she would've drilled down a bit further then she could've been profitable.

The key with selecting influencers is drill down far enough in a niche to make sure the audience is truly interested in what you're offering.

A sporting goods store.

A women's fashion brand.

An electronic store.

They all follow the same principle. Instead of looking for a gadget page, look for a page dedicated to HP laptops.

Finding the right Influencers.

To find the right influencers, you need to understand what you're selling and who you're selling to. For example, if you're selling sporting goods, you have a lot of different categories.

You have tennis rackets, basketballs, football cleats, etc. Each one of your products should be specifically targeted. Instead of searching for a page that deals with sports in a general sense, you'll need to find pages that deal with each one individually.

That means pages for tennis.

Pages for basketball.

Pages for football.

Pages for soccer, etc.

Use the Instagram search function and start with your keyword. For example, you'll start with basketball.

Type in basketball on the search page and click on the hashtag. Images you see will be the most popular pages related to that hashtag. Check them out to see if they're posting relevant content on their page.

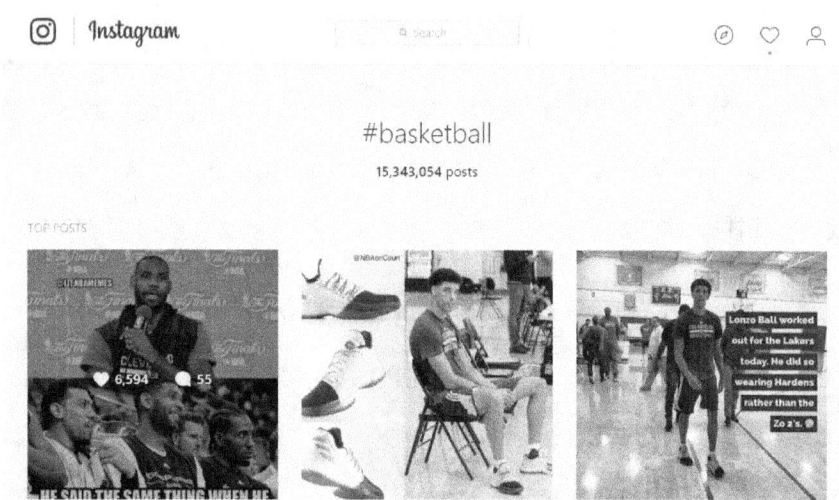

Once you navigate to the page, you'll look at whether they have readily available contact information, how many followers they have, and their engagement.

This is one of the pages I discovered using the process I outlined. You can as well follow them to discover new pages. That feature only works on mobiledevices. At the same time, the search process is better on mobile devices.

If everything checks out, go ahead and contact the page owner to see if they'll be open to promoted posts. If your follower numbers are close, you can pitch a s4s before asking for their rates.

How to Make the Most of your Influencer Posts

People get on social media for many reasons. They stalk their crushes, they spy on family members, and they interact with content that inspires them. It's hard to find the person that gets on the platform to shop.

Buying is a different frame of mind. There's a simple way to get over this obstacle. Don't make them buy.

I know what you're thinking, "What's the point in being on Instagram if I'm not going to make money from it?"

Instead of sending them to a page where they have to shell out $20, $50, $100 or more – send them a free product. Send them a free product and ask them to pay shipping. The free product is your front end offer. It creates a psychological shift from casual browser to paying customer.

Obviously, you'll need to be able to recoup a portion of your ad costs from the shipping. After they opt in to your free offer, you'll be able to upsell them into a more expensive relevant product.

This is where you earn your profit. Using this method, you'll be able to turn more Instagram users into customers and clients.

What kind of products and services can you offer at a discounted or even free rate? Do they lend themselves to upselling?

Could you offer a free 30 minute consultation call?

Chapter 13. The misconception about using Instagram for business

From the humble beginnings some years ago, Instagram has gradually metamorphosed into one of the best social media platforms for promoting business and brands with its hundreds of millions of active users.

Despite its dependence on photo sharing, it has become an able tool in the hands of good online marketers and has turned many businesses into a success.

However, some individuals and corporate bodies still see some limitations in its use as an effective marketing tool and have decided never to use the platform for their marketing. Well, you may have also heard about the limitations of the platform. If you have not, here are some of the most common misconceptions that are propagated about Instagram:

It is good for visual products only

This is perhaps the most popular misconception about the social media giant. This misconception has been branded so much that many people now take it as the basic truth. However, that is far from the truth.

While it is true that you can't post images of your brand or service if you are not into the sales of physical products, there are many ways a company can promote its services regardless. What can these companies show on Instagram? They can showcase some of these:

• Their merchandise

If companies can't post images of their services, they can make up for this by posting images of their merchandise. Since a company can have a long list of items, they can choose any one of them for posting on Instagram. Whether it is a hat with the company's logo, drink ware with the same feature, or any other merchandise, it represents that company and can be posted as a means of promotion. As a brand, don't be discouraged by the mindset that you can only post visual products. Let your merchandise play the role.

- Their culture

Each company has a culture. This culture shows what they're all about. They can post images of their culture as an indirect way of showing their services, although it is not physical. For instance, if a company shows an image of an award it had won, it will create awareness for others. Potential applicants will appreciate the image and may likely engage with the company.

It has also been noticed that images of customized desks of some companies also rank high on Instagram. Since they represent what the company stands for, it is an indication that people are still aware of the company, whether it offers a physical product or not.

- Their employees' generosity and goodwill

A company's employees are its ambassadors. When an employee is engaged in any goodwill or act of generosity, it can have a direct positive effect on the image of the company. Therefore, it is more than just a display of a personal act when a company shares the image of its employee's involvement in such an act. When a company shows images of its employees' caring attitude towards the community, the Instagram community will appreciate that. That is a plus for the employer. A constant uploading of such images will increase the popularity of the company. So, the goal of getting more viewers will still be achieved.

- Their moments

A common practice among companies is to celebrate some popular holidays, events, or their traditions. It is a big part of their culture and they can't afford to miss the opportunity to celebrate. These celebrations have turned into great opportunities turning their Instagram pages to their photo galleries. They do share their photos on Instagram and thus attract the attention of other users in the community.

It is meant for big brands only

It is the belief in some quarters that only big brands can succeed on Instagram. These people believe that if you don't have the financial power and huge followership to compete with the best brands in the world, you can't leverage the marketing power of Instagram. That is another blind misconception born out of complete ignorance to the operation of this social media platform.

The truth is that Instagram is not exclusively made for big brands. Small brands have benefited immensely from the marketing opportunities offered by the platform. Let me debunk that claim with the story of these small businesses that have found Instagram to be a viable tool:

- *Gordon Bennet:* This Israeli-based bicycle shop was the first in the country. The shop was formed to fit the needs of the bicyclists in the community. It is listed among the "14 Small Businesses that Really Know How to Instagram." That's right, because a bicycle shop doesn't fall into the category of big brands. As small as the bicycle shop is, it has over 2,000 active followers on Instagram.

- *Bon Puff:* This is another member of the 14 elite power users of Instagram. This small business brand specializes in making cotton candy. That doesn't fit into my definition of a big brand. Nevertheless, the company has over 24,000 followers on Instagram.

- *The Dog Matchmaker:* The Dog Matchmaker is another small business with over 2,000 followers on Instagram. The company is into the adoption of dogs and will link a dog with a potential home. By leveraging the power of Instagram, the company is a powerful stakeholder amongst dog lovers.

- *Fallen Industry:* This is a New York-based company and makes sculpture and furniture from fallen trees, hence its name. The fallen trees are then reclaimed by the company and then reborn to make beautiful sculptures and furniture.

With a little less than 8,000 followers, the company has been able to use Instagram to boost its business as most people around New York now patronize the company.

- *Wix*: Wix is a web development site for individuals and corporate organizations who want to create an amazing website without coding. The platform encourages these builders with its drag and drop tools that are easy to use and costs the users absolutely nothing except their time.

Wix can boast of having over 48,000 followers and is recognized worldwide among web designers and others in related fields.

None of the companies listed above qualifies to be called a big brand. Nevertheless, they are not discouraged by the negative mindset of some individuals who believe that Instagram is not meant for you if you don't have a big budget to spend on Instagram.

If you are a small brand and are contemplating using the Instagram for promoting your brand, go ahead and do just that. The platform is big enough to accommodate you alongside the big brands if you understand and play by the rules. You are never too small to book a space in the Instagram community.

It is for photo posting only

This is a misconception that is believed by a fair number of people and corporate organizations, big brands included. This assumption is based on the original purpose of the platform: photo-sharing.

However, the use of Instagram has grown beyond photo sharing alone; it has become a fantastic tool for brand promotion, whether you are a big brand or a small brand. The new role of Instagram as a promotional tool is based on its increasing popularity among social media users and its pro-business features.

There are other features of Instagram that you can use to get the best results. With the opportunity to organize special campaigns, leveraging the power of paid promotions, and organizing photo contests, you can do more than just post photos on Instagram.

You can't measure your results

Well, that was in the past. More innovations have made it possible for users to measure their results and understand the little tweaking they need to do to make better use of their time and resources on the platform.

With some tools like analytics, measuring your results on social media is very simple and effective. So, the propaganda is baseless. Some other tools you can use for analyzing your results include:

• *SumAll:* This is a New York-based cross-platform company that specializes in marketing analytics. The company offers a wide range of services which includes web traffic, social media, sales metrics, and some other services to make tracking your business and other social media metrics extremely easy. Within the span of 6 years, the company garnered over 500,000 users who are now reaping the benefits that the company has to offer. With this tool, you can measure the results of your Instagram efforts and see whether you are making any progress or not.

- *Iconosquare:* Iconosquare was formerly known as Statisgram. It is another analytics company that can help you to monitor and measure the results of your Instagram efforts to see how good you are doing. Iconosquare can be used in Instagram specifically for the following purposes:

- Use a single interface to manage your multiple Instagram accounts.
- Switch from one account to another effortlessly without closing your page.
- Create Instagram feeds that are customized to meet your personal needs and taste so that you will find it easy to follow some specific hashtags or some groups of Instagram users.
- Helps you to grow your account by giving you the tools you need to conduct a search for some users or hashtags in order to add to your customized feeds.
- If you have the latest media, Iconosquare has a feature that allows you to track all the comments you receive on that media.

- Make individual responses to comments. You can mark each comment after reading or delete any inappropriate comment. That helps you keep your account neat and compact.
- You can also measure your growth and make a prediction about your lost followers as well as gained followers.
- If knowing your what languages your followers use is important and can be helpful to you, this app will help you. In addition, it will also help you identify the locations of your followers.
- As a means of measuring your progress, Iconosquare allows you to measure whatever impressions and reach you achieve on your posts, profile, and stories.
- You can also track when your followers are most active on the platform. This is important if you remember that one of the best ways to increase your followership is by posting at the most appropriate time when your followers are active. With this tool, finding the best time for updating your account becomes very easy.
- You can also track the individual performance of any story or post.

- You can have a look into the performance of your posts in real-time so that you can make a useful comparison between those posts and previous ones.
- It is equally possible to measure engagement on comments, saves, likes, and video views.
- If some influential people are using your hashtags, you can easily identify them.
- Monitor your hashtag's growth.
- Identify your best performing posts.

These are some of the powerful ways that Iconosquare can help you easily monitor and measure the results of all your efforts on Instagram. That will be helpful in accessing your overall performance on the platform. You can make some useful deductions from the information you can gather when using the tool. That will contribute significantly to the growth of your account and increase your fan base drastically.

- *SimplyMeasured:* SimplyMeasured offers you an effective platform for simply measuring your progress on social media. The social analytics tool offers to provide you insight that you can find useful in creating, connecting, and converting your posts on social media. Some of its functions are:

- Listens to conversations so that you can easily discover influencers and emerging topics that you can then tailor to your needs for the purpose of reaching new audiences.
- Analyzes your social performance. The feature gives you free reign to explore your competitor's performance. The analysis may help you identify what you need to do to be on par with your competitors.
- You can also track content sharing on Instagram. That allows you to analyze the current trends on Instagram. Knowing what people are sharing on the platform, and during private conversations, will help you identify what is the common trend and how you fare in leveraging the trend.
- In addition to analyzing your competitor's benchmarks and campaign engagements, it also analyzes your audience growth.
- It also offers a cross-channel feature. This feature is useful in unifying data from Instagram, LinkedIn, Facebook, and YouTube accounts in order to gain insight from the reports.
- Finally, you can measure your social conversions. You can easily determine the impact of your

account on your purchases, leads, and other areas where you want your business to grow.

• *GramPro:* This is another good analytics tool at your disposal. You can use the tool to get comprehensive information about your Instagram account via posts, comments, likes, and other variables that can be used to measure your progress. Among other things, GramPro offers these services:

- Keeps track of gained or lost followers. The GramPro Stats features will give you a real-time analysis of your followership. That affords you the opportunity to have the number of followers you gain or lose at a specific point in time.
- What is more, it is also very easy to organize your followings or followers in a list. So, you can technically see how many of your photos were liked by your followers, how many comments do you have on those posts, what are the active level of your followers, and what is the country of residence for your followers.

This is valuable information you can gather by using GramPro. They will help you achieve your goal of building your followership and dispute some of the misconceptions about Instagram.

- *Static:* This app is another simple tool with a convincing efficiency if you want to keep up with your Instagram account and activities so that you can monitor your results. After adding your Instagram account to the app, it will be displayed on your main screen so that you can have a regular look into the strength of your follower base, the total number of your photos, and you're the number of Instagramers you are following too.

The Static app is cheap and can be purchased for less than $1. For that amount, you have everything you need to monitor your progress on a regular basis.

Therefore, it is a great misconception that you can't monitor your progress on Instagram. This falsehood has been debunked by the existence of these powerful and effective apps. If you have been discouraged all the while with this negative statement, it is high time you deleted that negative impression from your mind. You have the tools to do this. Period.

My product is too boring for Instagram

This is another powerful and highly influential myth that has discouraged some people from leveraging the benefits of Instagram for their businesses. Well, it may be true that businesses like food, lifestyle, fashion, and others that are visually-stunning will perform well on Instagram due to the glamour of such business niches. Does that mean there is no room for you if you are not in any of these fields? NO!

Instagram can offer you different avenues for marketing your product or services to the Instagram community to win their hearts, regardless of how "boring" some people want you to believe it is. While those business niches build their success on updating their accounts with product images, you can leverage some other features to build your account and followership too.

For instance, rather than follow the same trend and post what won't work for you, you can post images of your employees, the real people who are working tirelessly to make your company a success. A short video highlighting this will give you more followership if you do it right. That will work, even if you can't post product images.

You can borrow a leaf from Wells Fargo. This company deviated a bit from the norm by popularizing banking on Instagram and making the whole idea of banking less boring. How? The company uses a mixture of images and videos on their Instagram account to woo potential followers. The media cover some unconventional topics such as quotes, fun facts, and current events. What was the result?

 The result was a massive turnover from the Instagram community who fell in love with the new idea. That led to a big leap in the followership of the company. At the present, Wells Fargo has over 26,000 on Instagram.

So, your business is never boring and you can think out of the box and come up with some new innovations that can help you garner more followers rather than give up on your dreams due to some transient discouragement.

Let me talk about another company, Forever 21. Although this is a clothing company, some of the company's most engaging posts on Instagram have no connection with clothes. Over the years, this company has built a followership of over 9.5 million followers. Per image, the company has a record of almost 140,000 interactions covering comments and likes. You may then wonder how the company could record such figures.

For the record books and to the amazement of optimists, 65% of their best engaging posts did not contain accessories or clothes. Rather, four of the pictures portrayed painted nails, two images of skylines and desserts each, and other different posts with various themes. So, you don't have a boring product, you may just have a boring attitude.

You can't get direct traffic from Instagram to your website

Well, this is partially true. At present, you can't direct traffic to your website by sharing your link on your photo except when you purchase promotional ads. That makes it difficult to get direct referral traffic to your website. However, there is a way out of this problem. You can include the link in your personal or business profile bio. Then, you can include that information in some post captions so that Instagramers can view your profile bio to see the link to your website.

Whenever you have a new product or service to promote, you simply need to change the link in your profile bio to reflect the new promotion or marketing campaign. That way, you will get indirect referral traffic to your website from Instagram without breaking the site's terms and conditions.

It may be quite challenging to convince people to visit your website from Instagram. You'll need a convincing argument that is strong enough to make them to get off Instagram for a moment and check what you have in store for them. The most effective way to achieve that is by including a powerful call-to-action in your profile bio. That will trigger their curiosity and influence them to visit your website.

I will give you some practical tips that you can use to create an amazing bio that will woo any viewer to your page later in the book.

Chapter 14. Tips for successful Instagram marketing

There are ways that you can gain from all the benefits that Instagram offers. Some of these ways include:

Having a Great Profile

Your Instagram profile shows people who you are. By getting it right, you make yourself that much more appealing to your clients. Include contacts on your profile, which is possible with a business account.

From your user name to your bio, links and anything else on your profile, make it stand out. Also update it frequently, to avoid misrepresentation.

Offering excellent quality Content

Since Instagram is all about sharing visual images, you will need to ensure that your photos and videos are of excellent quality and creative. This sets you apart from the rest of the Instagram community, and attracts users to your feed.

Stay away from shabby photos and ensure the content represents your brand accordingly.

Being Consistent

Once you have excellent quality content, you also need to ensure that you are consistent with posting, and with the overall look of your profile. The color scheme of your feed should also be consistent, as it forms part of your brand and allows easier recognition from your followers.

Try to come up with a style that is unique to your business and stick to that style. This should include hash tags, color scheme, times of posting and such. Consistency makes your brand look more appealing to the audience.

Increasing User Engagement

This is one of the most important tips for great Instagram marketing. Optimizing user engagement lets you get more out of your account. You will need to use every technique possible to make sure that people are engaging with your posts.

Get people talking about your brand; whatever steps you take, ensure that you take the time to really engage with your audience.

When they leave comments, ensure that you respond to them, answer their questions, and you can simply tell them 'thank you'. Putting in effort makes the audience like your brand more, as they can relate with you. Do not take weeks to reply to questions asked; be as quick as possible to maintain a good reputation.

Also follow other users, like some of their posts and comment on them to further your engagement. And when you post photos, encourage the audience to leave comments on the posts.

Holding contests is another way of encouraging user engagement. These will also give you user generated content to post on your feed and allow testimonials from your followers who take part in your contests.

Influencer Marketing

This has gained traction over the years. You could incorporate it into your marketing strategy and further promote your brand in this manner.

By finding an Instagram account that has a lot of influence over many users, you could partner with them and pay them to market your products. You will need to find an influencer that has an audience you wish to target, that is preferably one in the same industry as you.

Influencer marketing gives you many people at your disposal to share information about your brand with and may increase your following as more users know of your existence through the influencers.

Furthermore, influencers tend to have an impact on the audience's choices. Having one promote your brand creates more trust for the user than if it was just you appealing to them.

Utilizing Instagram Ads

Instagram ads are a fantastic way to market your business if done correctly. They are made even better by the chance you have of targeting a specific audience based on geographic location, interests and such dynamics.

It does cost you, but the benefits far outweigh the costs in this case. Get your ad seen by users who do not follow you but fit your target description.

These are just a few tips to get you going on your efforts to use Instagram for marketing. There are very many techniques that you can use, but with these tips and a will to succeed, you will be on your way to actual success in just a short while.

Conclusion

We hope it was informative and able to provide you with the right advices to start building your social media empire into a prosperous business.

Now, you know how to create a profile that will grab and hold the attention of your target audience. You've also learned how to find your brand and build a following, and you've got all the tools to make your content beautiful, consistent, and unique. You can now start increasing your social media presence, upping your engagement rates, and building your brand into a booming business. Once you have a couple thousand followers, you can start reaching out to businesses using the helpful tips in this book and get a portfolio of product promotions under your belt to help you in future business partnerships. This book is a compilation of the tips and tricks that very successful influencers used to grow their brand into a business, and they can do the same for you!

Remember! Don't ever focus your attention only on the number of followers, instead consider the people as an interest audience, which cares about your content and actively interacts with you. Most of the time, smaller Instagram accounts are more profitable than the biggest ones, due to the fact that they can rely on a targeted audience with higher engaging rates.

Finally, if you found this book useful in any way, a review on Amazon is always appreciated!